P9-DNP-025

# A NOTE TO PARENTS

## Reading Aloud with Your Child

*Research shows that reading books aloud is the single most valuable support parents can provide in helping children learn to read.*

- Be a ham! The more enthusiasm you display, the more your child will enjoy the book.
- Run your finger underneath the words as you read to signal that the print carries the story.
- Leave time for examining the illustrations more closely; encourage your child to find things in the pictures.
- Invite your youngster to join in whenever there's a repeated phrase in the text.
- Link up events in the book with similar events in your child's life.
- If your child asks a question, stop and answer it. The book can be a means to learning more about your child's thoughts.

## Listening to Your Child Read Aloud

*The support of your attention and praise is absolutely crucial to your child's continuing efforts to learn to read.*

- If your child is learning to read and asks for a word, give it immediately so that the meaning of the story is not interrupted. DO NOT ask your child to sound out the word.
- On the other hand, if your child initiates the act of sounding out, don't intervene.
- If your child is reading along and makes what is called a miscue, listen for the sense of the miscue. If the word "road" is substituted for the word "street," for instance, no meaning is lost. Don't stop the reading for a correction.
- If the miscue makes no sense (for example, "horse" for "house"), ask your child to reread the sentence because you're not sure you understand what's just been read.
- Above all else, enjoy your child's growing command of print and make sure you give lots of praise. *You are your child's first teacher — and the most important one. Praise from you is critical for further risk-taking and learning.*

— Priscilla Lynch
Ph.D., New York University
Educational Consultant

Remembering Freya Littledale,
who introduced me to Buddy
— E.M.

To Juneau and Joshua III
— D.B.

Seeing Eye® is a registered trademark for dog
guides of The Seeing Eye, Inc. Only dogs trained
there are properly referred to as Seeing Eye dogs.

Text copyright © 1996 by Eva Moore.
Illustrations copyright © 1996 by Don Bolognese.
All rights reserved. Published by Scholastic Inc.
HELLO READER!, CARTWHEEL BOOKS, and the CARTWHEEL BOOKS
logo are registered trademarks of Scholastic Inc.

No part of this publication may be reproduced in whole or in part, or stored in a
retrieval system, or transmitted in any form or by any means, electronic, mechanical,
photocopying, recording, or otherwise, without written permission of the publisher.
For information regarding permission, write to Scholastic Inc., 555 Broadway, New
York, NY 10012.

Library of Congress Cataloging-in-Publication Data

Moore, Eva.
        Buddy, the first seeing eye dog / by Eva Moore ; illustrated by Don
Bolognese.
        p.    cm.—(Hello reader! Level 4)
        Summary: True account of the training and early work experiences of the
German shepherd which became the first seeing eye dog in America.
        ISBN 0-590-26585-7
        1. Buddy (Dog)—Juvenile literature.    2. Guide dogs—Training of—
United States—Juvenile literature.    3. Guide dog schools—United States—
Juvenile literature.  [1. Buddy (Dog)    2. Guide dogs—Training.    3. Dogs.    4.
Blind.    5. Physically handicapped.]    I. Bolognese, Don, ill.    II. Title.    III.
Series.
HV1780.2.M66      1996
[362.4'183— dc20                                                                    95-6725
                                                                                        CIP
                                                                                        AC

12  11  10  9  8  7  6  5  4  3  2  1                      6  7  8  9/9  0  1/0

Printed in the U.S.A.                                                                  23

First Scholastic printing, March 1996

# Buddy
## THE FIRST SEEING EYE DOG

by Eva Moore
Illustrated by Don Bolognese

Hello Reader! — Level 4

SCHOLASTIC INC.
New York  Toronto  London  Auckland  Sydney

# Chapter 1

## Gala and Kiss

Two dogs were playing in the spring sunshine. They were frisky, young German shepherds. They lived in a place called Fortunate Fields. It was in the mountains known as the Swiss Alps.

Many German shepherd dogs lived at Fortunate Fields. They were trained for important work. Some became police dogs. Some learned to deliver messages. Some were taught to find people who were lost.

A woman came walking up the hill. "Gala! Kiss!" she called. The dogs raced over to the woman. She was their owner, Dorothy Eustis. Dorothy was an American, but she had come to live and work in the Swiss Alps. She raised and trained the dogs at Fortunate Fields.

Gala and Kiss were almost old enough to begin their training. But they would not become police dogs or rescue dogs. They would not be like any other dogs born at Fortunate Fields. Something new was about to happen.

# Chapter 2

## The Seeing Eye

Over the years, Dorothy Eustis had come to admire German shepherd dogs above all other breeds. They were smart and loyal. They could be trained to help people in many ways. Dorothy had even seen pictures of a shepherd dog in Germany leading its blind master safely across a busy city street.

At first, Dorothy thought the pictures must have been faked. For hundreds of years blind people had depended on dogs to be their "ears." But how could a dog — even a smart one — be trained to act as a blind person's eyes?

Then Dorothy found out that there really was a school in Germany where shepherd dogs were trained as guides for soldiers blinded in battle. Dorothy had to see this for herself.

In the summer of 1927, she went to visit the school in Germany. There she followed a blind man and his dog as they took a walk along the wide city streets.

The dog had a special harness with a long, stiff handle. As the man held onto the handle, the dog steered him around lampposts, baby carriages, and other people in the street. They walked along so fast that Dorothy had a hard time keeping up.

When Dorothy got back to Fortunate Fields, she could not stop thinking about what she had seen in Germany. If only every blind person could have a dog like the ones she had seen! Blind people would no longer need to depend on others to get around. They could go to and from work on their own and not be afraid of crowds or traffic. Best of all, they would never again have to face the darkness alone.

# Chapter 3

---

# Something New at Fortunate Fields

It was a new year at Fortunate Fields. And for the dog named Kiss, it was the beginning of a new life. She and her playmate, Gala, were being trained for work as dog guides.

Dorothy had sent one of her best trainers, Jack Humphrey, to the school in Germany. When Jack returned, he knew how to teach a blind person to work with a dog.

Kiss was a good pupil. She quickly learned the most important rule: to obey. She learned to understand simple commands. *Sit. Come. Right. Left. Forward.* She learned to sit when she came to a curb so that her master could feel the edge and step down safely. She learned to walk around objects lying in the street. And she learned to make a wide path around low tree branches and other dangers above the ground, too. She learned to bark if someone came too close.

Now Kiss was ready to start work. She had been chosen to be Fortunate Fields' very first dog guide.

One day, Jack led Kiss into the large living room. A tall young man was waiting there.

"Here is your dog," Jack said to the man.

The man held out a piece of meat. Kiss's cool, wet nose touched the man's hand as she gobbled up the treat.

The man was Morris Frank.

Morris was blind. He had come all the way from America for a dog guide.

"What does she look like?" Morris asked Jack.

"She has a dark-gray coat with a creamy patch under her chin," Jack told him. "Her name is Kiss."

Morris moved his hands over the dog's body. He felt the strong shoulders and back. He patted her head, then got down on one knee and put his arm around her.

"Kiss?" he said. "That's a terrible name for a dog! I'm going to call you Buddy."

From then on, no one ever called her Kiss again.

# Chapter 4

## Lessons

Jack had spent many weeks training Buddy. Now Buddy would have to learn to obey a new master. The lessons began the next day.

Jack handed Buddy's harness to Morris. Morris ran his fingers over the long, U-shaped handle.

"That handle is the key to everything," Jack said. "When you hold the handle, you will be able to feel when Buddy slows down or changes direction."

At first the harness felt strange to Morris. "Pick up the handle with your left hand," Jack said. "The dog always works on your left side. Keep your shoulders back and walk fast, so you feel a pull on the handle. But don't expect Buddy to know where you want to go. You must tell her."

Now Morris had to learn to speak to Buddy in a voice she would obey. He also had to learn how to take care of Buddy—to brush her coat and fix her food—and how to put on her harness by himself. After all, he would have to do all this when he and Buddy were on their own.

# Chapter 5

## Buddy to the Rescue

Day after day, Morris and Buddy practiced walking around the grounds of Fortunate Fields. Then one day Jack said, "I think it's time for a real test. Are you ready to go into the village?"

Morris had been waiting for this day. "Let's go!" he said. He took hold of the handle of Buddy's harness and gave the command he had practiced many times: "Forward!"

Buddy and Morris marched down the hill to the gate. When they got there, Buddy stopped.

"What's the matter?" Morris asked Jack. "Did I do something wrong?"

"The gate is closed," Jack told him. "Buddy just did what she was supposed to do."

"Good girl!" Morris said, and gave her a pat.

Jack opened the gate, and the three of them walked on down the hill.

Every day after that, they walked from Fortunate Fields to the cable car that ran down the mountainside into the village of Vevey.

In town they walked along the twisting streets, with Morris giving directions and Buddy leading him safely through the traffic.

Morris was getting used to the feel of Buddy at the end of the handle. But sometimes he didn't pay attention to the signals she gave him.

One day outside the cable car, Buddy suddenly sat down. But Morris didn't stop. He came crashing down onto some steps.

Morris was angry with Jack for not telling him about the steps.

"I'm sorry if you hurt yourself, Morris," Jack said. "But you must learn to pay attention to Buddy at all times. Your life may depend on it."

One afternoon on the way home from the village, Morris and Buddy were making their way slowly up the mountain path. Jack was far behind them.

Suddenly Morris heard a wild clatter on the road above, and the sound of horses' hoofbeats pounding the ground. Two horses had broken away from their wagon and were running straight toward Morris!

Buddy tugged with all her might as Morris gripped the harness handle. He

found himself being pulled up a steep, rocky slope along the side of the path. In the next second, he felt the runaway horses rushing past him.

Morris fell to his knees and reached out for his dog.

Jack came running up. He had barely gotten out of the way himself. "That was a close call," he said. "Lucky for you, Buddy has learned her lessons well. She saved your life!"

# Chapter 6

## "I'm Free!"

By the end of May, Morris knew every twist and turn of the village streets. He could tell where he was from the sounds and smells in the air.

One day Morris and Buddy went into Vevey alone. "Forward!" Morris commanded, and Buddy led him along the main street. Now Morris could hear the clucking of hens. He knew he was near the poultry shop on the corner.

"Left!" he said to Buddy. Before long Morris smelled fresh loaves of bread. They were passing the bakery. "Good," he said to himself. "We're going the right way."

Then came the sweet smell of soap and bay rum. "Stop, Buddy," Morris commanded. "Right!" Buddy led him to the barbershop. She waited as Morris had his hair cut.

When he got back to Fortunate Fields, Morris sat down in the living room with Buddy at his feet. Suddenly he laughed out loud.

"What's so funny?" Dorothy asked him.

Morris said, "Ever since I was sixteen, someone has had to take me to the barbershop. I've been left there for hours at a time, waiting to be picked up. Today I went out and got my own haircut and came right back home." Morris laughed again. "Now I'm sure I am really going to be free. That's why I'm laughing—I'm free!"

It was time for Morris to take Buddy home to Nashville, Tennessee. She would be the first dog guide in America. But she would not be the last—not if Dorothy and Morris had their way. They made plans to start a new school for dog guides in the United States.

It would not be easy. Buddy would have to prove to Americans that a dog could be the eyes of a blind person.

# Chapter 7

## Buddy's Biggest Test

The trip across the Atlantic Ocean took seven days. Buddy made a lot of friends on the ship. Even the captain took a liking to her and invited Morris to bring her up to the captain's deck. No other dog had ever been given this honor.

Just before they were due to land in New York, Morris had to trade his foreign money for American dollars at the ship's office. But as he went to slip the wallet back into his pocket, he missed. The wallet fell to the floor without a sound.

Morris turned toward the door of the office. "Forward, Buddy!" he commanded. Buddy obeyed. But first she picked up the wallet in her mouth.

It was a long walk from the office to Morris's cabin. Buddy held on to the wallet as they went up and down stairs and along the narrow hallways.

Morris was tired when he got to the cabin. He lay down on the bed. But Buddy kept tapping his arm with her paw.

"Stop it, Buddy," he said. "Let me rest."

Then Morris felt Buddy put her forefeet on the bed. Something fell onto his chest.

"My wallet!" he said. "I must have dropped it. But you knew it was important." He gave Buddy a big hug. "Good girl. You mean more to me than any amount of money."

Buddy's biggest test came right after the ship docked in New York. As usual, there were newspaper reporters at the dock looking for good stories to print in their papers. When they heard about Buddy, they crowded around Morris. They asked him all kinds of questions.

Morris told them about Buddy and the school for blind people that he planned to start. It would be called The Seeing Eye. Some of the reporters didn't believe it was possible for a dog to lead a blind person.

"If your dog is so good," one reporter said, "why don't you show us? I dare you to cross West Street. It's the street right here in front of you."

"Okay," said Morris.

Morris had no idea how dangerous West Street was. It was very wide — more than twice as wide as any street in the village of Vevey. And it was busy, with traffic going in two directions.

But Morris was eager to show off his wonderful dog. He gave the command, "Forward, Buddy!"

All was quiet when Buddy stepped off the curb and started across. Then West Street suddenly sprang to life. Cars and trucks came speeding toward them.

Buddy pulled back on the harness, and Morris stopped. He felt a whoosh of hot air as a truck zoomed by, right in front of them.

But there was no turning back. Buddy started forward again. To Morris it was like walking into a wall of sound.

Horns honked. Brakes screeched. Drivers yelled. Buddy stopped and stepped forward so many times that Morris lost all sense of where he was. It seemed like the longest walk he and Buddy had ever taken.

At last, Morris felt the curb, and stepped up onto the sidewalk. His heart was pounding hard as he leaned over to give Buddy a pat.

"Good girl," he said. "Good, good girl!"

"She sure is!" someone said. It was the reporter. "I had to take a taxi to get here myself," he told Morris. "And some of the other guys who tried to cross with you didn't even make it. They are still back on the other side of the street!"

Morris and Buddy spent a few days in New York. Reporters and photographers followed them on their walks.

On his trip down to Nashville, Morris stopped in two other cities — Philadelphia and Cincinnati. Everywhere they went, people stared at the proud young blind man and his wonderful dog guide.

# Chapter 8

## The Seeing Eye

Back in Nashville, Morris's life was much different now. With Buddy, he could go anywhere in the city on his own. He liked to be with his friends, but he was glad that he no longer had to depend on anyone else to help him get around.

He made his living by selling insurance from door to door. Now that he had Buddy, his business was better than ever before.

Stories about Morris and Buddy were printed in newspapers around the country. Morris began to get letters from other blind people. They wanted to know about The Seeing Eye. When was it going to open? How many students would there be?

Back at Fortunate Fields, Dorothy and Jack were training more German shepherds as dog guides. Buddy's playmate, Gala, was already prepared. Jack brought her and another dog, Tata, to Nashville in December. Dorothy came in January to help raise money for the school. Finally they were ready. The first two students began their lessons in February 1929.

The classes got bigger each month. More dog guides were trained so that more students could enter the school. Blind men and women walked in feeling helpless and

alone. Three weeks later, they walked out with their "seeing eyes," proud and ready to enjoy life on their own.

After two years, The Seeing Eye was still growing. But the summers in Nashville were very hot. Dorothy, Jack, and Morris decided to go north. In the fall of 1931, Morris and Buddy moved to New Jersey. The new school was to open near Morristown at the end of the year.

# Chapter 9

## Buddy, the Pioneer

In October of 1936, Buddy turned ten years old. That morning there was a party at the school. Everyone sang "Happy Birthday to You" as the birthday cake was brought in. The cake was made of tasty meat and

crunchy dog biscuits, with ten candles made of butter. Buddy ate the candles first. She loved butter.

Later, Morris and Buddy met with newspaper reporters. Flashbulbs popped as the photographers took pictures of "the birthday girl."

Morris liked all the attention. He was always glad to have a chance to tell others about his special "lady," his best friend, his Buddy.

The next year the newspapers had more news about Buddy—news that made all her friends sad. Buddy had become sick. She had to have an operation. But the operation did not cure her. A few months later, in the spring of 1938, Buddy died.

It was hard for Morris to say good-bye to his dear companion. He thought of all the years they had been together. He thought of all the times he had put on her harness and commanded, "Buddy, forward!"

On the day of Buddy's funeral, Morris put on her harness for the last time. He wanted her to be buried with it because, he said, "It was the way she was always happiest."

After Buddy died, Morris Frank got another Seeing Eye dog. He named her Buddy II.

Morris had four more dogs after that. He named them all Buddy. He loved all his dogs. But the first Buddy would always be special. She was a true pioneer. Like the pioneers who settled the wilderness, Morris and Buddy had opened the door to a new way of life. They had made life easier for blind Americans who came after them.

Today The Seeing Eye in Morristown, New Jersey, matches about 300 blind people with its specially trained dogs every year. About half the dogs are German shepherds and half are Labrador retrievers and other breeds. If you would like a comic book that tells about The Seeing Eye program, write to:

> The Seeing Eye
> P.O. Box 375
> Morristown, N.J. 07963-0375

*Photo of Morris Frank and Buddy I courtesy The Seeing Eye®, Inc.*